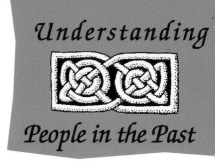

Understanding

People in the Past

SERIES EDITOR: SYDNEY WOOD

The Changing Highlands
Clearances and Crofting

IAIN JOHNSTON

Hodder & Stoughton

A MEMBER OF THE HODDER HEADLINE GROUP

INTRODUCTION

This book will help you to understand the changes which have affected people's lives in the Scottish Highlands from the seventeenth century. It will help you to understand the causes behind the Clearances and emigration. It will also enable you to see how these changes affected crofting communities and allowed the Highlander to influence the heritage of other countries, such as Canada, Australia, New Zealand and America. The book will help you to achieve this by using a variety of different sorts of evidence and explaining how useful the different sorts of evidence are.

The traditional Highland world of clanship was coming to an end well before the Battle of Culloden. Highland chiefs had increasingly come into contact with Lowland Scotland and England after 1603. The chiefs were quick to realise that the world which was emerging was one where money played a very important part. From the 1760s, we see some Highland chiefs trying to increase the amount of money earned from the land by breaking up the old townships and creating single farms with sheep or cattle.

The outbreak of war with France in 1793, along with the growing towns of Lowland Scotland and England, meant a ready market for clothing and food. Sheep were ideally suited to the Highland landscape and introduced from this time to a great extent. In some areas, such as the Outer Isles, kelp manufacture from seaweed was introduced. Both changes resulted in clearances of the people to crofting communities on the coast. In the 1850s, further clearances occurred. This was cheaper than to have a poverty-stricken crofting population remain, after the potato famine of 1846. Further sheep farms and then deer forests for sporting purposes followed.

You will find out about the difficulties of life on the coast in a crofting community, the experience of emigrating, the reasons for the crofters' war in 1882 – 1888 and the findings of a government enquiry in 1884. You will also look at the effects of the Crofters' Act 1886, along with improvements and continuing difficulties in the twentieth century.

We can still see the effects of these dramatic changes in the Highlands around us today. You can visit the sites of clearances, museums, have a quick look at the number of Highland names in a Lowland Scotland telephone directory, or observe the many tourists who come to the Highlands of Scotland because their ancestors once lived there. The Scottish Highlander has made a permanent impact on the life of Lowland Scotland and the world.

I hope this book will stimulate your interest and encourage you to find out more about the Highlands of Scotland. Above all, I hope you enjoy finding out!

Contents

Did you know that about 20 million people in the world today have Scottish ancestors? This is because many Scots have gone to other countries, to start new lives. One in every 10 Australians has a Scottish name!

When people leave to live their lives in another country, we say that they have 'emigrated'. To find out where Scots have emigrated to, the historian needs evidence. These pages show you some of the evidence you can use.

▼ **Source 2**

You can find this church on the island of Madeira, in the Atlantic Ocean. Madeira is part of Portugal. The people who built this church left a clue as to which country they had come from. Which country was it? The answer is to be found above the entrance gate!

This is a cost-shared project constructed with the assistance of the Nova Scotia Department of Fisheries.

Government of Nova Scotia

▲ **Source 1**
Flag of Nova Scotia.

This is the official flag of the area in Canada called Nova Scotia. It clearly shows that most of the people living in this part of Canada have Scottish ancestors. Can you work out why?

▼ **Source 3**
Road sign, Cape Breton.

There are many road signs like this one in Cape Breton, Nova Scotia, Canada. This part of Canada has a large number of people with ancestors from the Highlands of Scotland. Can you find two things from the road sign which tell you this?

Australia	E. MacKenzie
New Zealand	S. Gordon
Canada	S. Stewart; C. Stewart; G. MacKinnon
Zimbabwe	E. MacMillan

These players played for their country in the 1991 Rugby World Cup.

Source 5 is a memorial to those who fought and died in the Second World War, from the village of Mabou in Cape Breton.

Look at the surnames in Sources 4 and 5. Where exactly did the ancestors of most of these people come from?

▼ **Source 5**
Memorial to World War II dead from Mabou, Cape Breton.

▼ **Source 6**
Centres of Scottish settlement in Australia and Canada.

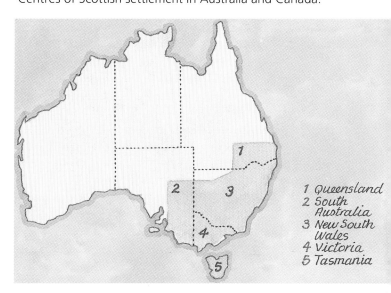

1 Queensland
2 South Australia
3 New South Wales
4 Victoria
5 Tasmania

Hudson Bay

Quebec

Upper Canada

1 Pictou (Nova Scotia)
2 Cape Breton Island
3 Prince Edward Island
4 Quebec
5 Toronto
6 Red River Settlement
7 St. Lawrence River
8 Montreal

1 You will need maps of Canada, Australia and New Zealand. Work with a partner to find as many place names, rivers, mountains and anything else which suggest the names were given by Scottish emigrants.

2 Once you have listed all your names, work out with your teacher which names were given by emigrants from the Scottish Highlands.

A C T I V I T I E S

2 Upheaval in the Countryside

Hello! My name is John Cockburn of Ormiston, East Lothian. I lived between 1679 and 1758. During that time I 'improved' my estate. This meant many changes. I ended the old runrig system of agriculture. Instead, I gave compact farms, the sort you would recognise today, on long leases to single tenant farmers. These farms were enclosed by hedges and trees to keep any animals out. I encouraged the growing of new crops such as clover, rape, turnips and artificial grasses. Turnips in particular provided winter feeding for the animals. I sent the sons of my tenants to England, so they could learn the newest ideas in agriculture. I also rebuilt the village of Ormiston itself. Here, I encouraged new industries, including the making of linen from the flax grown by my tenants and whisky and beer from their barley.

This is how John Cockburn of Ormiston may have explained the improvements on his estate.

▲ **Source 1**

Hello! I used to be a tenant farmer on the estate of John Cockburn of Ormiston. Like many others in the time of the old townships, we farmed the runrig land together. Now that the old township is gone and runrig farming ended, I can't afford the money to bid for a lease on one of the new farms. I have a number of possible choices. I can become a wage labourer on one of the new farms, go and work in one of the nearby new industries like the coal mines in Tranent, or go to one of the rapidly growing Lowland towns or cities, such as nearby Edinburgh.

This is how a Lowlander may have looked at his situation with the coming of enclosed farms.

▶ **Source 2**
Plan of the runrig system.

In the old runrig system of farming, the rigs could be from 5.5–6 m (18–20 feet) wide and 183–457 m (200–500 yards) long. They were swapped around between farmers after one, two or three years, to ensure everyone received a fair share of good and bad land. The areas between the rigs were often covered in weeds. Ploughing, using oxen and a traditional plough, was slow and inefficient.

The main crops were oats and bere (a type of barley). Soil exhaustion was a problem because these crops drew nitrogen from the soil. No other crop was widely used to replace this lost nitrogen. The size of crops at harvest was often poor. This meant a lack of winter feed, such as turnips, for animals. Sheep and cattle were small and thin as a result. There are stories of cattle being carried out of byres in the spring because they were so weak. Most were killed and eaten or sold at Martinmas (11 November). There was no selective breeding because animals could wander at will.

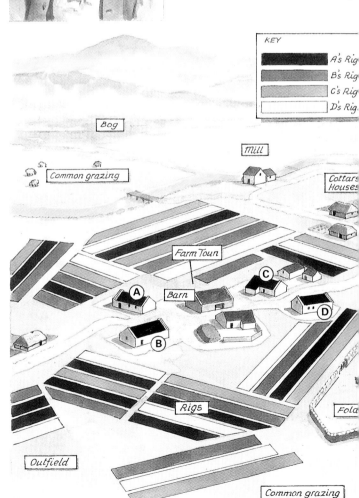

KEY

A's Rig
B's Rig
C's Rig
D's Rig

Bog
Common grazing
Mill
Cottars Houses
Farm Town
C
A
Barn
D
B
Rigs
Fold
Outfield
Common grazing

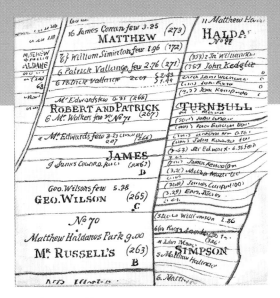

▲ **Source 3**
Plan of enclosures at Tranent in East Lothian.

In Source 3 a number of names have been printed in large block capitals above others. The names in block capitals are those of the new tenant farmers. The names in small print are the former tenants working runrigs. The new tenant farmers received a much larger farm from putting the old runrigs together, to make 'enclosed' fields. Regions differed in size and type of farming. New breeds of sheep, the Linton and Cheviot, appeared in large-scale sheep farming in the Moorfoot Hills. Sheep farming reached those areas of the Highlands bordering the Lowlands (Perthshire, Morvern and Southern Argyll) by the close of the eighteenth century. Sir John Sinclair also introduced Cheviot sheep to Caithness in 1792.

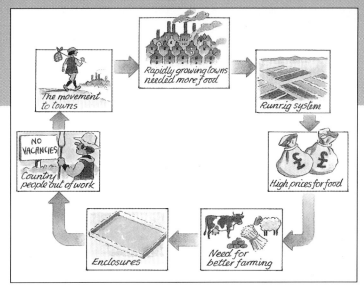

▲ **Source 4**
Connection between changes in agriculture, industry and population.

By the close of the eighteenth century, textiles (cotton, woollen and linen goods) were the main industries. Charcoal, coal and iron were all increasingly needed for the new factories and growing town populations. Many landowners had also tried to encourage manufacturing in newly planned villages, when they enclosed their estates. Distilling was established in Dufftown, fishing in MacDuff and tourism in Ballater. There were almost 400 planned villages. Earlier in the century, many Glasgow merchants made vast fortunes from the tobacco trade with America.

▼ **Source 5**
Distribution of Scotland's main industries at the close of the eighteenth century.

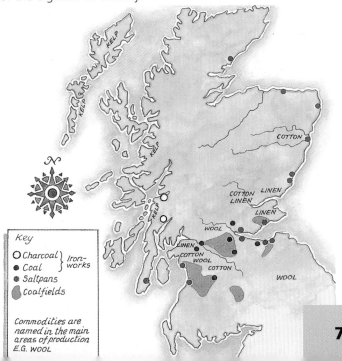

ACTIVITIES

1 Look at Sources 1, 2, 3 and 4. Make a list of the changes brought about by the move from runrig farming to enclosed farms. There are lots! You might want to make your list under the headings of:

   land layout   *crops used*
   new animals   *planned villages*
   what happened to the people

2 Use Sources 4 and 5 to explain why there was a need to change the system of runrig farming.

Change in the Highlands

In the late seventeenth and early eighteenth centuries, Scotland was repeatedly troubled by fighting. This usually heavily involved many Highland areas. The cause of all this trouble was a difference of opinion about who should be king. On one side were the Jacobites, who supported the House of Stuart, and on the other those who supported William of Orange and his successors from the House of Hanover, George I and George II.

▼ ▶ **Source 1**
Different points of view.

> I don't like the Jacobites because the kingdom should be governed by a Protestant ruler. The Catholic James VII threatened my Protestant religion, power and status when he was king. Those areas of Scotland which are developing in trade and commerce are mainly Protestant. A Protestant ruler will guarantee continued economic development, progress and prosperity.

This sums up what a Jacobite supporter may have thought. The Jacobites took their name from the Latin 'Jacobus', for James. There were Jacobite rebellions in 1689, 1708, 1715 and 1745 - 1746, but each ended in failure.

> I am a Jacobite. I support the House of Stuart because they are the rightful kings. James Stuart (James VII) was king until 1689. In this year, William of Orange came from Holland to seize the throne and James fled to France. William of Orange had no right to do so. I agree with other Catholic and Episcopalian clans that we should try to restore a Stuart king to the throne, by force.

▼ **Source 2**
The Battle of Culloden was over in less than an hour. The government forces lost around 300 men, the Jacobites lost about 2000!

The Battle of Culloden shows that the Jacobite rebellion of 1745 - 1746 was a civil war in Scotland. There were Scots and Highland clans on both sides. Even families were divided in their support. William MacIntosh supported the government, but his wife, Lady Anne, supported the Jacobites. Some clansmen such as MacKenzies, MacLeods and Chisholms came out to fight despite their chiefs' wishes.

The failure of most chiefs to support the rising is evidence of the changes affecting the Highlands through the seventeenth and eighteenth centuries. Most Highland chiefs had growing business and trade interests. The Highland chiefs were becoming more like the landed classes of the rest of Scotland and England. They feared losing all. You will find out more about how the role of Highland chiefs changed in Chapter 4.

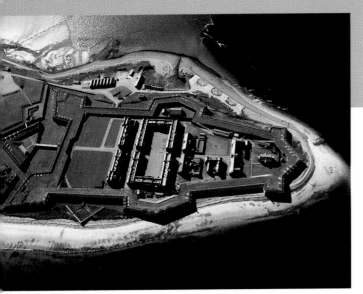

▲ Source 3
Fort George.

Fort George was built between 1748 and 1769, at Ardersier outside Inverness, to show government power in the Highlands. More military roads were also built.

The private courts of the chiefs were banned and no land was to be held for military purposes.

The Crown seized 41 rebel estates: 28 were sold to pay off debts and 13 were put under the control of government officers.

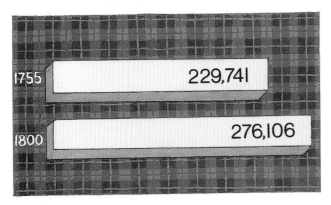

| 1755 | 229,741 |
| 1800 | 276,106 |

▲ Source 5
Highland population, 1755 – 1800.

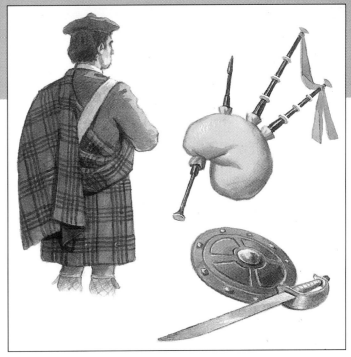

▲ Source 4
The government took extreme measures to destroy clanship in 1747, banning highland dress, bagpipes and carrying weapons.

The population of the Highlands between 1755 and 1800 rose by over 20 per cent. The potato had been introduced to the Highlands in the 1740s. By the 1780s it was a main part of the Highland diet. Smallpox inoculation from the 1780s also meant fewer deaths.

The 13 estates taken over by the crown after Culloden provided a model as to how to 'improve' the Highlands in a time of growing population. Old clan townships were broken up and given to one person (single tenant), planned villages were built and crofting communities made on the coast from the people who had been 'cleared'. This was the model used by Highland lairds from the 1780s. By then, the relationship between chiefs and clan had well and truly changed.

1 From the information on these pages, make a timeline of the main events affecting the Highlands between 1689 and the 1780s. You should be able to take 'at least' one event from each source. You should also use drawings beside each of your entries.

2 Which event do you think was the most important for the Highlands? Give reasons for your answer. Discuss your choice with the rest of your class.

A C T I V I T I E S

Changing Chiefs

In English, the word clan means the children. The traditional role of the Highland chief was to offer protection, kindness and justice to the clan, in much the same way as a good father would. The land occupied by the clan was not farmed for profit, but as a means of growing crops for survival. The status (importance) of a Highland chief was measured by the number of men he could call upon in time of conflict.

By the early eighteenth century, a change in attitude, towards both land and people, can be detected among the Highland chiefs. They were quickly becoming part of the British landowning class. They regularly travelled outside the Highlands, perhaps to Edinburgh, London or in some cases on a grand tour of continental countries. Highland chiefs were starting to think of their clan and the land they occupied as a means of paying for their increasingly expensive lifestyle.

Alasdair MacDonnell of Glengarry, the 15th Chief, had this painting of himself done by a famous artist (Source 1). MacDonnell was responsible for evicting his clansmen from the 1770s until his death in 1828, by which time the Glengarry estates were almost bankrupt. Why do you think this chief was so keen to have a painting of himself?

Highland chiefs increasingly wanted to copy the lifestyle of the rest of Scotland's wealthiest landed class, during the seventeenth century. They did not escape the criticism of the Gaelic poets of the time, who could be found among the clans.

Roderick Morison's poem, a 'Song to MacLeod of Dunvegan', severely criticised this Highland chief's new lifestyle. Other poets made similar criticisms of their chief.

▼ **Source 1**
Painting of Alasdair MacDonnell of Glengarry.

▼ **Source 2**

SONG TO MACLEOD OF DUNVEGAN

...He comes out of the shop with the latest fashion from France, and the fine clothes worn on his person yesterday with no little satisfaction are tossed into a corner ... When he returns to view his own country, though thousands of pounds have already been sent away, a cattle levy is imposed on the tenantry. Thus do the debts increase to be demanded from his son after him.

Everything is turned upside down since you left Lochaber ... Families who have not been disturbed for four or five hundred years are turned out of house and home and their possessions given to the highest bidders. So much for the Highland attachment between chief and clans.

This was written to an emigrant tacksman in Canada in 1804, by the son of another tacksman still in Lochaber.

The chiefs' increasing debt meant they were more interested in activities which would make them money. The Highland black cattle droving trade grew rapidly as a result.

By the Jacobite rebellion of 1745, the clan chiefs had substantial business interests. Cameron of Lochiel had interests in tobacco, grain, timber, black cattle, trade with the West Indies, Boston, Philadelphia and New York, in addition to smuggling wines from France!

▼ **Source 4**
This is a traditional Highland township. There were many tenants. This system of farming was really only designed to produce enough food for everyone to survive on.

1. The Duke of Argyll was the first chief to break up traditional townships. He did this to the townships of Mull, Morvern and Tiree. In 1737 most of the townships were leased (rented) to the highest single bidder.

2. From the 1760s, other chiefs broke up their traditional townships to give them over to single tenant sheep farmers. The 'Clearances' had started.

3. Wool and mutton could clothe and feed the growing Lowland and Southern population and, from the 1790s, the army and navy fighting against the French.

4. In the Western Isles, single tenant farms were first of all designed to make much greater profits from tending cattle.

5. By the close of the eighteenth century there was a 'rage for emigration'. This was due to the break-up of traditional townships.

The chiefs were now treating the land and people as property.

1 From Sources 1 and 2 describe what sort of person the Highland chief had become. You should use examples from the sources to help explain your answer.

2 How useful is Source 3 for finding out about the changing values of Highland chiefs?

3 From Source 4, explain what the consequences were for the Highlands of the chiefs' changing attitudes to land and people.

A C T I V I T I E S

The Coming of the Crofter

By the 1820s, communal townships with many tenants had been replaced by single sheep farmers as the only tenants. The result was the formation of crofting communities for the people who had been removed.

▼ **Source 1**
The crofting areas of Scotland.

■ Main crofting areas

▨ Areas with scattered crofts

0   km   80

▼ **Source 2**
The crofting township of Boreraig from the estate map of the Clan Donald estate, Sleat, Isle of Skye.

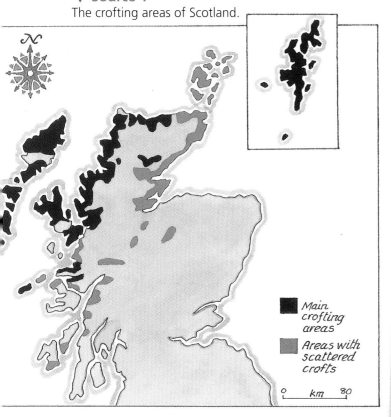

This shows an estate map from 1811, for the crofting township of Boreraig, on the Isle of Skye. Each of the 8 crofts, 1 per family, was allocated a specific amount of land. The land was laid out in strips, something which you can still see in crofting communities today. The families had access to some further grazing for animals.

▼ **Source 3**
There were a number of differences between crofting and the old runrig system of communal townships:

- the land on the coast was exceptionally poor for growing crops;
- crofters could not survive from the land alone;
- crofters were expected to combine working on the land with another occupation. In most crofting areas this was either fishing or kelp making (see Chapter 10). In some places, however, planned villages were built, such as Grantown-on-Spey. The intention was to encourage industry and manufacturing.
- the available hill grazing, for the crofter's cattle, was often very limited because the sheep occupied all the best land.

There is a great deal of evidence to show that, from the 1780s, crofters increasingly worked away from home for part of the year doing seasonal work. This could be on Lowland farms at harvest time, the new industries growing up in the Lowlands or the East Coast fishing. Others are recorded as having served in the merchant navy, for years at a time. Young women worked as domestic servants (maids) in the houses of wealthy Lowlanders.

▲ Source 4

(Above Left) Skye peasant with the caschrom (foot plough) and (Above right) Skye woman with peat creel.

These illustrations come from the Illustrated London News, 15 January 1853. Peat was used as fuel for heating.

▼ Source 5

My croft is about three acres [1.214 hectares] of very shallow land. I have no horse. We and our wives do the ploughing and harrowing [seeding] of our land, turning or tilling it with the caschrom.

With more families sharing the hill pasture and cutting peats on it, hill grazing is scarce and people suffer badly ...

A single Aberdeenshire cow would weigh more than three of ours. The amount of milk our cows give is very meagre.

Above our beds comes pattering down the rain, rendered dirty and black by the soot on the ceiling,

The description in Source 5 was given to the Napier Commission enquiry in 1883 (see Chapter 15) by a crofter from Glendale, Skye.

▼ Source 6

The walls were five feet thick, formed of an outer and inner casing of rough boulders, the centre being filled in with earth.... The roof was formed of rough cabers [poles] and spars [rafters], and on these was laid turf covered over with straw permeated with soot, so that it could be used for manure in the spring. The interior of the houses is generally in two portions, one part being used as a stable for livestock, and for the storage of manure, and the remainder as a living place for one family. The bed was often used as a roosting place for the hens, and he had seen a typhoid patient and the hens in the bed together ... a fire was generally burned in the centre of the house. The houses were generally without a window.

Source 6 is from a report about conditions in the Outer Hebrides in the nineteenth century.

Imagine you have been transported back in time to an early crofting community. Use the sources to make a list of things you might not be looking forward to!

A C T I V I T I E S

6 Clearances

The clearance of rural populations was not just a Highland event during the second half of the eighteenth century. A change of land use also affected the rural populations of the Lowlands of Scotland, England, the German states of Pomerania and Brandenburg, Denmark, Catalonia in Spain and the Low Countries.

The Highland lairds argued that the clearances were unavoidable. For them, it was a straight choice. If they didn't make more money from the land, bankruptcy would result. What made the Highland experience different from elsewhere was the sheer power of the lairds (landowners) over both the land and people, combined with the speed with which clearance occurred. In Sutherland from 1807 to 1821, between 6,000 and 10,000 people were cleared!

As historians we need to be open-minded and judge each clearance, for which there is written evidence, critically. Only then can we decide whether any particular clearance was just brutal, or that some concern for the future welfare of the people was shown. Having an opinion based on evidence is a key lesson to learn from studying history.

▼ **Source 1** ▶

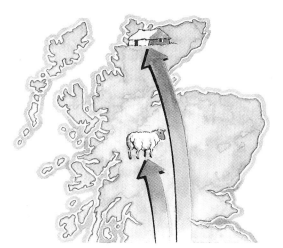

After the 1760s, sheep farming spread into the Highlands. The people were cleared. The crofting community where the people survived from combining working on the strips of croft land and some other occupation such as fishing or making kelp (see Chapter 10) was born.

The growing town populations of Lowland Scotland and England meant a ready demand for clothing (wool) and food (mutton) from Highland sheep farming.

With war against France, between 1793 and 1815, there was an even greater demand for wool and mutton. Prices rocketed and huge profits could be made by Highland lairds. At the start of the nineteenth century prices had risen to between 250 and 400 per cent more than in the 1770s.

War with France also meant a growing market for kelp, which is used in the manufacture of glass and soap. Large numbers of crofters were employed in the making of kelp during the wars against France because no similar materials could arrive from abroad. Kelp manufacture became big business especially in the Outer Isles, in places like South Uist. At the end of the war, kelp prices and demand collapsed and from the 1820s onwards large sheep farms started to appear in the Outer Isles.

The Highlands of Scotland may sell at present, perhaps £200,000 to £300,000 worth of lean cattle each year. The same ground will produce twice as much mutton, and there is wool into the bargain. If covered with course woolled sheep, the wool might be worth about £300,000 whereas the same ground under the Cheviot ... will produce at least £900,000 of fine wool.

Sir John Sinclair wrote this in 1795. He owned estates in Caithness.

▼ Source 3

Sir, Enclosed you have a list of small tenants belonging to my Knoydart property – their leases being expired by Whitsunday first – and having refused to serve me (in a Highland Regiment), I am fully determined to warn them out, and turn them off my property, without loss of time [a list of the tenants' names followed]

Alexander Macdonnell, Chief of Glengarry, wrote this to his agent in Inverness, November 1794.

Flora Robertson or Matheson, a widow, aged 96 years ... had a small lot of land in Suishnish. Her son was a widower, with four children; and shortly before the time for evicting the people arrived, he went away to labour at harvest in the south, taking his oldest boy with him. The grandmother and the other three children were left in the house ... The poor children ... thought no one would interfere with an old creature of 96 ... The officers, however, arrived and threw out before the door every article that was inside the house, and they placed large bars and padlocks on the door! ... a sheep-cot being near, the children prepared to remove the old woman to it. True, it was small and damp, and it had no door, no fire-place, no window, no bed, but then, it was better than exposure to the night air ...

(Three months later in December) ... I have no hesitation in declaring that she was then actually starving. She had no nourishment, nothing whatever in the way of food but a few wet potatoes and two or three shell-fish.

An eye-witness account from the clearance of Suishnish, Isle of Skye, 1853, by Donald Ross. He was a Glasgow lawyer and anti-landlord.

1 What evidence can you find in Sources 1 and 2 to support the view that the clearances were an economic necessity for the lairds?

2 Explain how Source 3 demonstrates the enormous power of the Highland lairds.

3 How useful is Source 4 for the historian wanting to find out whether the clearances were brutal or not? In your answer you should:

- think about who wrote this and when;
- explain why this is important;
- explain what the source tells you;
- provide an overall comment on whether it is possible to know about all clearances and lairds from one source only.

A C T I V I T I E S

The Trial of Patrick Sellar

▼ **Source 1**

The crimes of which Mr Sellar stands accused are:

1 Wilful fire-raising; attended with most aggravated circumstances of cruelty, if not murder.

2 Throwing down and demolishing a mill, also a capital crime.

3 Setting fire to and burning the tenant's heath pasture, before the legal term of removal.

4 Throwing down and demolishing houses, whereby the lives of sundry [several] aged and bed-ridden persons were endangered, if not actually lost.

5 Throwing down and demolishing barns, kilns, sheep-cots, etc., to the great hurt and prejudice of the owners.

6 Innumerable other charges of lesser importance swell the list.

In June 1814, Patrick Sellar was in charge of evictions in Strathnaver, Sutherland. Sellar was the owner of a new sheep farm in this area, at Rhiloisk, and factor to the landowner, the Duchess of Sutherland. Soon after the evictions, the duchess received complaints from the removed tenants. At Inverness High Court, in April 1816, Sellar was found not guilty on all charges. The jury took fifteen minutes to reach their verdict.

Robert McKid, Deputy Sheriff of Sutherland, wrote Source 1 in May 1815. McKid was not asked to give evidence at Sellar's trial. There is some evidence to suggest that McKid personally disliked Sellar for private reasons.

▼ **Source 2**

I have always known him to be a man of sympathy, feeling, and humanity (good deeds).

I think him incapable of being guilty of the charges brought against him.

The above are quotes from letters read out in court by Sellar. They were all written by members of the same social class as Sellar. This was also true of the jury who tried Sellar. The jury was made up of 15 men. It included 8 landowners, 2 merchants, 2 tacksmen and 1 lawyer.

▼ **Source 3**

The more I see and hear of Sellar the more I am convinced that he is not fit to be trusted further than he is at present. He is so exceedingly greedy and harsh with the people, there are heavy complaints against him from Strathnaver.

The Duchess of Sutherland wrote this in a private letter. James Loch, her Commissioner, wrote back that Sellar, 'was really guilty of many very oppressive and cruel acts'. A recent historian wrote in 1981 that 'The picture of Sellar resorting to force is unproved and at odds with his known character.'

Donald MacLeod, eye witness to the evictions wrote this:

> *I was present at the pulling down and burning of the house of William Chisholm, Badinloskin, in which was lying his wife's mother, an old bed-ridden woman (Margaret MacKay) of nearly 100 years of age, none of the family being present. Mr Sellar came. On his arrival, I told him of the poor old woman being in a condition unfit for removal. He replied, 'Damn her, the old witch, she has lived too long; let her burn.' Fire was immediately set to the house, and the blankets in which she was carried were in flames before she could be got out. She was placed in a little shed, and it was with great difficulty they were prevented from firing it also. She died within five days.*

William Chisholm was called to give evidence at Sellar's trial. Like the other five witnesses, he only spoke Gaelic. Neither he nor the others were wearing smart clothes. Sellar called Chisholm a thief and bigamist [a man with more than one wife] during the trial. Sellar was not asked to prove either charge.

The Reverend Donald Sage wrote this account (Source 5) of Sellar's conduct of evictions in Strathnaver in 1814, in a private diary. This was published in 1889, by his son.

▼ Source 5

> *The poor widow had to address herself to the work of dragging her sheets, beds, presses and stools out at the door, and placing them at the gable of her cottage. No sooner was her task accomplished than the torch was applied and the widow's hut speedily ignited. The wind unfortunately blew in the direction of the furniture and the flame, lighting upon it, speedily reduced it to ashes.*

▼ Source 6

> *... if the jury were at all at a loss on this part of the case, they ought to take into view the character of the accused; for this was always of importance in balancing contradictory [disagreeing] testimony.*

Source 6 describes how the judge, Lord Pitmilly, summed up the case before the jury's decision. The judge said all charges, except two, should be ignored. One was the testimony of William Chisholm and the other concerned the destruction of barns. The judge thought this destruction ignored a custom of the country, but did not break the law of Scotland.

There is no record of Sellar's trial, apart from what was written down by a member for his defence. This did not record the arguments used by those trying to prosecute Sellar.

Gaelic tradition refers to 1813 as *bliadhna na losgaidh* (year of the burning). One Gaelic poem, recorded in Prince Edward Island, Canada, refers to Sellar burning homes and hopes that, at his death, his body will be flung on a dung heap. Sellar's son published a book in 1883 in which he denied that his father was responsible for any atrocities. What do you think?

Work as a group. Imagine you are a jury member at Sellar's trial. You have to decide whether Sellar is guilty or not, 'beyond reasonable doubt'. Use the information in the Sources to help you make your decision. Present the findings of your group to the rest of your class.

A C T I V I T I E S

By the late eighteenth century, the Highland chief was part of the British landowning class. He was a laird, who thought of the land and people as property. The purpose of this property was to provide profit. As such, the people possessed no rights. Anything that was done to bring about 'improvement' (more money) was therefore justified, even if this included 'clearance'. For the laird, changes to Highland society were just a plain economic necessity. Moreover, the sorts of changes themselves, like the introduction of sheep and kelp making (see Chapter 10) were brought about by events outwith the laird's control! This is of course looking at events from a laird's point of view.

▼ Source 1

By the close of the eighteenth century, towns and cities were growing rapidly in Lowland Scotland and England. This population had to be fed.

Land and climate in much of the Highlands were not suitable for raising crops in the huge amounts needed to feed the growing UK population. Neither did the Highlands have large deposits of natural resources, such as coal, or large urban centres. The ways in which the Highlands could contribute to the new commercial world of Britain was therefore very limited.

I am a Highland laird. I have no choice but to introduce sheep to my estate. Sheep will provide food and wool to clothe the growing population.

I too am a Highland laird. I can get the people to make kelp, which is in great demand.

Could lairds argue when people were cleared that this had been brought about by forces outwith their control?

Both the lairds and government wanted to keep the people on the estate because, by the late eighteenth century, Britain was involved in many wars. For every recruit the lairds received a government payment. The laird could also show his importance to other landowners by the number of recruits raised.

Crofting townships on the coast meant the people would grow crops but also have to fish as well. This would create more money than the old system of runrig agriculture which did not produce much in the way of crops to sell.

The adoption of sheep pastures is most advantageous to the people themselves.

The improvements ... have had constantly for their object the employment, the comfort, the happiness of every individual who has been the object of removal; and there is no single instance of any man having left this country on account of his not having had a lot [croft] provided for him.

James Loch, estate manager on the Sutherland estates from 1813, wrote this in 1820.

▼ Source 3

Francis Clerk was laird of Ulva, Mull. He gave this evidence to a government enquiry in 1851. What evidence can you find to suggest that he tried his absolute best for his tenants? How could Francis Clerk argue that he had to clear many of his tenants because he had no other choice?

I have personally managed my own property from the time when I purchased it, and to enable me the better to do so, I have acquired the Gaelic language... In the first years after the failure of the potato, I purchased meal, I borrowed money and I have also expended more than £500 in draining and other improvements, from my own private funds, chiefly with the view to give employment to the population; but finding that the crofters could not pay their rents, and that my private resources were therefore diminishing from year to year, I had no alternative but ... very reluctantly resolved to promote the removal of the crofters, and proceeded to warn off a certain number yearly.

▼ Source 4

Dr. J. MacCulloch wrote this in 1824. He was an annual visitor to the Highlands and stayed at various lairds' houses.

the former hamlets [traditional townships] of the idle and useless population ... The attachment of the wretched creatures in question was a habit; the habit of indolence [laziness] and inexperience, the attachment of an animal little differing in feeling from his own horned animals. They were children, unable to judge for themselves, and knowing nothing beyond the narrow circle of their birth, it was the duty of their superiors [lairds] to judge for them and to compel them for their own advantage.

Most historians now agree that the majority of ministers at the time neither spoke out against the clearances, nor encouraged opposition to it from the people. Can you think of a reason why the reaction of most Church ministers would have made the lairds feel better about Clearance?

Were the lairds right? What could be said in their own defence? Use the information and sources to answer the following.

1 Put together a list of reasons, explaining why the lairds thought that the changes they introduced to Highland estates were justified.

2 Explain whether you are convinced by the lairds' arguments. Give your own reasons for why you think this.

ACTIVITIES

The Crofters' Case

The Highland lairds and gentry, of the late eighteenth century quickly became part of a new commercial and business world (see Chapter 4), interested in money and profit. The traditional values of ordinary clan members was much slower to change. The crofters did not share the Highland laird's view that clearance was an improvement over the old traditional way of life.

The evidence left by the crofters themselves tends to record the actual experience of clearance. In some cases this was brutal. You will have to decide for yourself, whether the way individual clearances were carried out could have been achieved less harshly. Neither does this evidence take account of whether landlords had any option but to 'clear' the people, to avoid bankruptcy.

As a historian you should:

- Look at events with an open mind;
- be alert to possible 'bias' in the evidence;
- realise that everybody's experience was not necessarily the same!

▼ **Source 3**

Description of the eviction of Elizabeth Gillies, aged 60, tenant on the Glengarry estate in 1853.

Widow Gillies was sitting inside her house when the factor and officers arrived. ... she was ultimately thrust out at the door, from where she creeped on her hands and feet to a dyke side, being quite exhausted and panting for breath, owing to the hard struggle with three powerful men. Whenever they got her outside, the work of destruction immediately commenced. Stools, chairs, tables, cupboard, spinning-wheel, bed, blankets, straw, dishes, pots, and chest, were thrown out in the gutter ... they set to work on the walls outside with picks and iron levers ... When I visited Knoydart I found the poor widow at work repairing her shed ... She said it was indeed most ungrateful on the part of the representatives of [the laird of] Glengarry to have treated her so cruelly – that her predecessors were, from time immemorial [beyond the reach of memory], on the Glengarry estates – that many of them died in defence of, or fighting for, the old chieftains – and that they had always been true and faithful subjects.

▼ **Source 1**

▼ **Source 2**

Donald MacLeod recorded the events of clearance in Sutherland in the early 1800s.

I was an eye witness of the scene ... I myself ascended a height about eleven o'clock in the evening, and counted two hundred and fifty blazing houses ... [and it] ... lasted six days ... During one of these days a boat lost her way in the dense smoke as she approached the shore; but at night she was enabled to reach a landing place by the light of the flames!

▼ **Source 6**
An account by General Stewart of Garth, 1822.
He was sympathetic to the Highlanders.

▼ **Source 4**

A Gaelic poet wrote this at the time of the introduction of large-scale sheep farming to Highland estates.

> *Destruction to the sheep from all corners of Europe! Foxes and eagles for the lambs! I have overlooked someone, the Factor! May he be bound by tight thongs, wearing nothing but his trousers, and be beaten with rods from head to foot. May he be placed on a bed of brambles and covered with thistles.*

> *When the valleys and the higher grounds were let to the shepherds, the whole population was driven to the sea shore, where they were crowded on small lots of land, to earn their subsistence [living] by labour and by sea fishing ... over the whole of this district, where the sea shore is accessible, the coast is thickly studded with wretched cottages, crowded with starving inhabitants ... Ancient respectable tenants, are now pining [starving] on one or two acres of bad land, with one or two starved cows... when the fishing fails, they fall in arrears [debt] and are sequestrated [bankrupted], and their stock sold to pay the rents, their lots given to others, and they and their families turned adrift on the world.*

▼ **Source 5**
The Bays district of Harris.

Source 5 shows the Bays of Harris. Most of the population of Harris were cleared to here by the 1850s. The rocky landscape meant the people had to grow potatoes on lazybeds. The Bays area was used in the film 2001: A Space Odyssey, because it resembles the landscape of Jupiter!

1 In what ways does Donald MacLeod's account (Source 2) of the Clearances in Sutherland differ from that of James Loch in the previous chapter?

2 Do you think any part of MacLeod's account is exaggerated? Explain your answer.

3 Why did Elizabeth Gillies (Source 3) find it so difficult to understand why clearance was necessary?

4 Look at who the poet blames in Source 4. How does this support the view that old feelings of loyalty to the Highland chiefs were very slow to disappear, despite the clearances?

5 Do Sources 5 and 6 support the idea of 'improvement'? Give reasons for your answer.

ACTIVITIES

▲ **Source 1**
Ullapool, Wester Ross.

This is modern-day Ullapool, Wester Ross. It was originally one of several planned villages, designed to encourage the fishing of large herring shoals. A government agency, the British Fisheries Society, helped fund its construction in 1788. The idea was to encourage the crofters to be dependent upon both land and fishing.

Some success did occur, but by the 1820s herring shoals were in decline. There was also increasing competition from much larger East Coast boats, such as those from Aberdeen and Fraserburgh. These places attracted many seasonal workers from the Highlands. On a much smaller scale, local fishing continued to be important for crofters.

Some crofting areas on the coast were quite suitable for fishing. Orkney is perhaps a good example. The British Fisheries Society, however, had only invested in a few villages. Much of the money they spent wasn't even on boats and equipment. For crofting areas on the coast which were not so suitable for fishing, a lack of money and resources proved a real problem.

Donald MacLeod from Rossal in Sutherland wrote this. He had been cleared and emigrated to Canada.

▼ **Source 2**

William McKay, a respectable man, shortly after settling in his allotment on the coast, went one day to explore his new possession, and was suddenly swept away by a splash of the sea, from one of the adjoining creeks, and lost his life, before the eyes of his miserable wife, in the last month of her pregnancy, and three helpless children who were left to deplore his fate. They had no harbours where they could land and secure their boats in safety, and little or no capital to procure [buy] sound boats, or to replace those which were lost. In one year on the coast, between Portskerra and Rabbit Island [about 30 miles], upwards of 100 boats had been either totally destroyed or materially injured, so as to render them unserviceable; and many of their crews had found a watery grave!

Landlords also saw the profit to be made from the manufacture of kelp. The kelp was obtained from seaweed collected between April and August. It was cut and left to dry in the sun and wind. It was then burned in stone kilns filled with peat. The bluish material left at the bottom of the ashes [kelp] was collected and sent south. It was made into soap and glass.

▼ **Source 3**

Growth of population (%) in kelp-producing areas, 1755 – 1811.

Place	Percentage of growth
North Uist	102
South Uist	118
Harris	81
Barra	84
Lewis	58
Mull	81
Skye	31
North West Mainland (including Ardnamurchan & Morvern)	76

▼ **Source 4**

A nineteenth century traveller in the Highlands wrote this:

If one figures to himself a man, and one or more of his children, engaged from morning to night in cutting, drying, and otherwise preparing the seaweeds, at a distance of many miles from his home, or in a remote island; often for hours together wet to his knees and elbows; living upon oatmeal and water with occasionally fish, limpets and crabs; sleeping on the damp floor of a wretched hut; and with no other fuel than twigs or heath; he will perceive that this manufacture is none of the most agreeable.

▼ **Source 5**

Lord MacDonald's factor reported this in 1839:

The fall in the value of kelp renders … a change in the management of the North Uist estate necessary. The population of the estate is greater than the land, the kelp being abandoned, can maintain. The allotments of land held by the small tenants are so small that they cannot maintain their families and pay the proprietor the rents which the lands are worth if let in larger tenements. It becomes necessary, therefore, that a number of small tenants be removed; [and] that part of the estate calculated for grazings be let as grazings.

1 Many crofters became involved in seasonal work. Use Source 2 to help explain why such work was necessary, to pay the rent.

2 Donald MacLeod wrote a book on the Clearances from stories he heard and collected from other people. He was himself evicted from Rossal in Sutherland and emigrated to Canada. Why does the historian need to be careful in using evidence such as that in Source 2?

3 Look at Sources 3 and 4. Why was there such a huge population increase in the kelp-producing areas?

4 How valuable is Source 5 for understanding the reasons for large-scale emigration after the collapse of the kelp industry?

ACTIVITIES

Famine

Potato farming in the Hebrides.

Unlike places such as Canada, Sweden, Belgium and Denmark, the crofting population of the Highlands could not turn to other crops or afford to buy other foodstuffs, in the event of a potato crop failure. In August 1846, the potato crop in the Highlands was stricken.

▼ Source 3
Norman MacLeod visited the Outer Isles in August 1847 and witnessed the effects of the famine.

This photograph was taken in the later part of the nineteenth century. It shows the crofter's method of planting potatoes. The woman's basket is full of seaweed carried from the shore. The seaweed was used to help fertilise a very poor quality soil for growing crops.

In the mid-1840s, a killer fungus struck the potato crop of Europe and North America. The fungus (Phytophthora infestans) was unknown to people at the time. They could take no action to prevent its spread. The potato quickly became a mass of rotten pulp.

We know from a government report in 1843 that the potato was the main item in the diet of the majority in the Highlands and Islands.

The scene of wretchedness which we witnessed as we entered on the estate of Col. Gordon was deplorable, nay heart rending. On the beach the whole population of the country seemed to be met, gathering the precious cockles ... I never witnessed such countenances [expressions] – starvation on many faces – the children with their melancholy [sad] looks, big looking knees, shrivelled legs, hollow eyes, swollen like bellies – God help them, I never witnessed such wretchedness!

▼ Source 2
Quotation from an account by R. Somers, 1846.

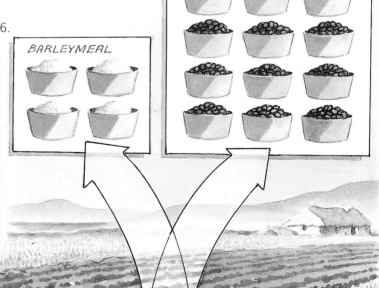

POTATOES

BARLEYMEAL

If planted with potatoes, crofts were of great advantage to families, but their produce was insignificant if sewn with corn or with barley – a piece of land that used to yield 12 bolls* of potatoes has returned 4 bolls of barleymeal; but 3 bolls of barleymeal, or 2 bolls of oatmeal, for 12 bolls of potatoes, is a much more common return.

* A boll of meal is 140lbs; a boll of potatoes is 448lbs

	Date	Description	Location
1846	October	'Much sickness of the cholera class . . . attributed to inferior diet, namely, bad potatoes.'	Raasay
	December	Number of deaths from dysentery and British cholera 'increasing with fearful rapidity among the cottar class.'	Throughout the Hebrides
1847	February	'Fever, measles and influenza are very distressing on south end of Harris . . . no persons are employed there or are allowed to go near the sickly districts.'	Harris
1848	April	151 of population sick with fever and smallpox.	Skye
1847–9		'much diarrhoea'	Gairloch

Reports such as these came in from all over the Highlands after the failure of the potato crop. The government did not believe in giving anything away for free, even to the starving. They introduced a 'work test', before the starving could receive food handouts.

Building walls, quays, drains and roads were the sorts of work Highlanders could perform in return for food. Unfortunately, this was to the benefit of the landlord's estate and not the crofter's holding.

There were fewer deaths in the Highlands of Scotland compared to Ireland, because of a number of important differences. By the 1840s, there was much more interest in Highland affairs from outside. The heroic deeds of Highland Regiments and the writings of Sir Walter Scott were known internationally. Contributions to fundraising came from Scots the world over, including the Free Church in the Lowlands of Scotland. Cargoes of relief, such as grain, could be shipped quickly using the new powerful naval steamships. Seasonal migration to the Lowlands and East Coast fishing (Chapter 5) were also available in the 1840s. The first burst of railway building in the Lowlands helped at this time too.

The discovery of gold in Australia offered emigration as a solution for both landowners and crofters.

▼ Source 5

The test of destitution [poverty/starvation] consists in the exchange of eight hours time and a moderate amount of labour for a ration of 7 lbs meal [oatmeal] per week for the party himself; by a corresponding increase of the labour test, he may receive ten and a half per week. His acceptance of either of these tests entitles him to a daily allowance of half a lb of meal per child in his family; in addition there is extended to the wife the opportunity of spinning or knitting, calculated to allow from three quarters to a pound of meal per day, Sunday included.

1 Look at Source 2 again. Why did the Highlanders rely so heavily upon the potato?

2 From Sources 3 and 4, describe, in your own words, the health problems brought by the failure of the potato crop.

3 Read Source 5 again. Do you agree that the 'work test' was a fair measure? Give reasons for your answer.

ACTIVITIES

12 New Owners, Visitors and Image

Between 1820 and 1860 many Highland estates were sold to new owners. After the end of the wars against France in 1815, the kelp industry collapsed, cattle prices fell and the returns from fishing were very poor. Highland landlords faced bankruptcy and financial ruin. Debts had to be repaid, so estates were sold to wealthy Lowlanders and Southerners. Such people were only too willing to buy Highland property. It was cheaper than to buy an estate elsewhere in the UK. Land ownership also gave status.

For some new owners, it was a chance to make fast money. They believed that the first step towards this was the eviction of most of the people, often brutally.

An interest in all things Highland developed by the middle of the nineteenth century, for reasons other than just financial.

▼ Source 1

CHORUS

Will ye no come back again?
Will ye no come back again?
Better lo'ed ye canna be,
Will ye no come back again?

This famous song was written by Lady Carolina Nairne (1766 – 1845). The threat from Jacobitism was dead, but the appeal of Bonnie Prince Charlie and the Highlands was quickly becoming 'romanticised'. Many Lowland Scots were prepared to believe in a fictional history, in order to find a national identity. This allowed them to show that they were different from the English, but still could enjoy the benefits of being British, as well as Scottish.

The exploits of the Highland regiments (see Chapter 16) brought fame and respect to the Highland soldier the world over. Writers such as James MacPherson turned the Highlander into a 'noble savage'; a fighter with all the qualities of an ideal subject. Such qualities of manners, loyalty, bravery and courtesy were becoming increasingly valued, in the fast-changing cut and thrust of the new urban world of nineteenth century Scotland. Many started to believe that all Scots had once been like these Highlanders.

This is a portrait of George IV by David Wilkie. As monarch, he came to Edinburgh in 1822, dressed in full Highland costume. The identification of all things Highland with Scottish was made. Many wealthy Lowland Scots quickly tried to find their own tartans.

▼ Source 2
George IV.

Queen Victoria loved the Highlands. It was peaceful, appeared unspoiled and the people seemed so courteous. She had Balmoral Castle built in 1855. Queen Victoria more than anyone else helped identify tartan, the Highlands and Scottishness. The drawing room at Balmoral had a tartan carpet. She, her husband and children all wore kilts. Her support for Highland dress and Highland games firmly established the popularity of both. Queen Victoria's presence in the Highlands also helped stimulate tourism.

By the mid-nineteenth century the Highlands were attracting tourists such as sightseers, artists, botanists and geologists.

▼ Source 3

The Inverness Advertiser of 4 August 1857 gave this report:

Thomas Cook Tour

Summer Excursion

One of Mr Cook's annual excursion trips to the Highlands took place last week. The party consisted of about fifty ladies and gentlemen, who came here on Tuesday afternoon by the Caledonian Canal and left next morning by the Highland Road, both Mr Grant's coaches in Dunkeld having been engaged for the purpose. Another trip, we understand, is fixed for the 1st of September, when Mr Cook intends bringing a party of a hundred persons from the South by the same route. He has engaged five coaches to convey the party by the Highland Road.

By the 1840s there was also a steamboat service from Oban up the West Coast. By the 1860s, railway travel was a further possible means of getting to the Highlands.

Many of the rich became interested in deer hunting. Some were visitors. Others bought estates to develop them as deer forests. The Marquis of Salisbury bought the island of Rhum, in 1845, for this purpose.

▼ Source 4

Deer forests in the Highlands and Islands c. 1850.

Deer forests

1 Look at Sources 1 and 2. What evidence can you find from the sources to support the view that the Highland image quickly became the make-believe Scottish national identity, by the mid-nineteenth century?

2 Do you think that Queen Victoria would have had a balanced view of life in the Highlands or did she just see the lifestyle of the wealthy? Explain your answer.

3 What evidence can you find from Source 3 to support the view that tourism was increasing in the Highlands?

4 What do you think were the attractions of deer hunting for the wealthy? Discuss your answer with your teacher and the rest of your class.

A C T I V I T I E S

Changing Culture

By the middle of the nineteenth century, whole areas of the Highlands had converted to the Protestant religion. A few areas such as Barra and South Uist did not. Presbyterianism was the religion of the Lowlands of Scotland. It did not believe in the priests of Roman Catholicism or the bishops of Episcopalianism.

Protestantism was seen, by those who believed in it, as the religion of progress, civilisation and personal improvement. These were all qualities which the government, chiefs and Lowlanders quickly came to believe the Highlands were in great need of. They were convinced of this need by the Jacobite Rebellions by Episcopalian and Catholic clans. At the heart of this Highland problem, so it was thought, was the Gaelic language and the need to learn English.

All chiefs and gentry in the Hebrides were supposed to send their eldest children to learn English in Lowland schools. To those outwith, the Highlands appeared an alien culture from an early date.

The Society in Scotland for Propagating (spreading) Christian Knowledge was founded in 1709. Its schools in the Highlands taught English and the Protestant faith. It was thought this would destroy loyalty to Jacobitism and the House of Stewart.

Highland chiefs in the seventeenth century had greater contact with the landed classes of Protestant Lowland Scotland and England, who all spoke English.

By the beginning of the nineteenth century many Protestant missions had gone to the Highlands from societies which were founded in English-speaking Scottish cities and towns.

The Church of Scotland was keen to make inroads to the Highlands to achieve conversion to Presbyterianism.

Lay preachers also emerged from the crofters themselves. They were known as *Na Daoine* (the Men). Lowland missionaries had taught them to read. In the Gospels which talked about land, the crofters found much they could relate to. So intense were these prayer meetings that there are recorded cases of people taking fits, spasms and fainting.

The crofters had little in common with the Church of Scotland ministers who appeared close to the landlords and in some cases were even sheep farmers. *Na Daoine* believed that the suffering of the people would be rewarded in heaven, at which time landlords could also be expected to be judged!

The beliefs of *Na Daoine* meant old customs had to end. John Farquharson of Skye is seen burning his fiddle here, in 1805. Dancing was also prohibited.

In 1843 the Church of Scotland split. A new Protestant church emerged, the Free Church of Scotland. Most of the crofting population joined this church, especially as it had been so active in trying to relieve suffering during the potato famine of 1846.

▼ Source 2

In May 1845, the people of Glencalvie spent a week living outside in the courtyard of Croick Church, after having been evicted. They etched on the window panes. 'Glencalvie people the wicked generation.'

▼ Source 3

By learning to read and to understand that he [the pupil] reads in his native tongue [Gaelic], an appetite is generated for those stores of science [learning] which are accessible to him only through the medium of the English language.

▼ Source 4

The Reverend Alexander Stewart, 1812.

The isle of Barra: the Gaelic is the only language commonly spoken here, though by their frequent excursions to Glasgow, the people have introduced a number of English words. Numbers of the inhabitants, who attended the school, speak English tolerably well.

These accounts were both written by parish ministers in the 1790s.

1 Look at Source 1. In no more than 30 words, explain what the main changes to Highland culture were by the middle of the nineteenth century.

2 How do we know from Source 2 that the Highlanders were deeply religious? (Give a reason for your answer.)

3 From Sources 3 and 4 give three reasons why the usage of the English language spread amongst the Gaelic-speaking Highlanders?

4 Look back at Chapter 12, what other developments by the mid-nineteenth century would have increased the usage of English speech in the Highlands?

A C T I V I T I E S

The Crofters' War

The 1880s was a period of conflict between crofter and landlord. At the heart of this was a very different view about land ownership.

▼ Source 1

The earth is mine . . . the earth is the Lord's and the fullness thereof . . . Woe unto them that join house to house, that lay field to field . . . The earth he has given to the children of men.

The crofters believed God had granted the land to the people, but the landlords at the time of the Clearances had taken this away from them. Now they wanted the land back. As can be seen from this quotation, the crofters thought their beliefs were supported by the Bible: see Isaiah 5: 8.

▼ Source 2

I think they [the people] have as much right to my common as I have to their clothes; the land is mine, and their coats and hats are theirs, and I cannot see how they can claim the pasture. It never did belong to them.

This is what General Burroughs, an Orkney landowner, said in 1884.

There was good reason why trouble erupted in the early 1880s. There was an economic slump, after relatively good times in the 1860s and 1870s. The potato crop failed, while gales ruined the grain crop. Severe weather destroyed many fishing boats and the number of fish caught was very poor overall. Payment for working at seasonal jobs, in the Lowlands, was also much lower than in recent times.

The crofters were well aware that an Irish Land Act had just been passed in 1881. This had granted fair rents, security of tenure (occupation without the threat of eviction) and the freedom to inherit a landholding. Highland crofters also realised that this had been achieved by tactics such as refusing to pay rent.

▼ Source 3
The Battle of the Braes (Isle of Skye).

▲ November 1881: Braes crofters present a petition to Lord MacDonald's factor to have grazing rights restored on Ben Lee. The petition is rejected.

▲ The crofters march a few days later to the factor's office in Portree. They tell him, 'that their rents would not be paid that day, or any other day, until Ben Lee was returned to them'.

▲ By April 1882 Lord MacDonald had taken out eviction notices against 12 Braes crofters for non-payment of rent.

▲ 7 April 1882: A sheriff officer from Portree was set upon by a crowd at Braes. His eviction notices were burned.

▲ 19 April 1882: The Sheriff of Inverness-shire William Ivory and 50 policemen arrive in Braes. Extra police had been called in from Glasgow. Sheriff Ivory was at the rear!

▲ 'The Battle of the Braes.' Those who burned the eviction notices are arrested. Other crofters try to release them. Police and women are injured.

▲ The police escape with their captives. The crofters received light fines, which were paid by sympathisers.

Rent strikes spread throughout Skye and elsewhere in the Highlands. During the winter of 1883 – 1884, land raids took place on South Uist, and Lewis.

By mid-November 1884, there were 300 marines on Skye. There were no pitched battles. The crofters just ignored them.

Land raids continued after The Crofters Act of 1886. Land raids were led in Lewis and Assynt, Sutherland, by the cottars who had gained nothing from this Act. However, the government may have sensed that public opinion was now less sympathetic to the crofter. It may have appeared that the Act of 1886 had solved the Highland problem. The government could afford to give out harsher prison sentences, which they did to those Lewis cottars taking part in the Aignish land raid, 1888. This served as an example to all.

Conditions were also improving after 1886. Cattle prices recovered, as did the fishing. The Crofters Commission set up under the 1886 Act to establish fair rents also reported in January 1887. Many rent arrears were written off and rents did indeed appear to be fairly set. In September 1888 troops withdrew from Lewis. The Crofters War, if not Highland problems, had come to an end.

Enquiry and Reform

▼ Source 1

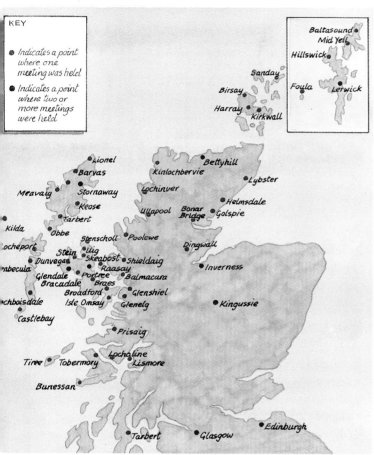

KEY

● Indicates a point where one meeting was held

● Indicates a point where two or more meetings were held

Baltasound
Mid Yell
Hillswick
Sanday
Foula
Lerwick
Birsay
Harray
Kirkwall

Lionel
Barvas
Kinlochbervie
Bettyhill
Lybster
Meavaig
Stornaway
Lochinver
Keose
Helmsdale
Ullapool
Bonar Bridge
Golspie
Tarbert
Kilda
Obbe
Poolewe
Stenscholl
Dingwall
ocheport
Stein
Uig
Skeabost
Shieldaig
Dunvegan
Raasay
nbecula
Glendale
Portree
Balmacara
Bracadale
Braes
Inverness
Broadford
Glenshiel
chboisdale
Isle Omsay
Glenelg
Castlebay
Kingussie
Prisaig
Lochaline
Tiree
Tobermory
Lismore
Bunessan
Edinburgh
Tarbert
Glasgow

This is a map showing the places at which the Napier Commission held meetings.

In the early 1880s, there was growing unrest in the crofting areas (Chapter 14) and increasing public sympathy for the crofter. This led the government to establish The Napier Commission. Under Lord Napier as chairperson, this group toured the crofting areas between May and December 1883. They held 71 meetings, in 61 places, and heard evidence from 800 crofters.

The Commission's purpose was to find out about the conditions in which the crofters and cottars (landless or near landless) lived. It has provided a goldmine of information about nineteenth century Highland life.

▼ Source 2

Angus Stewart, a crofter from the Braes area of Skye, told the Commission this:

I want the assurance that I will not be evicted, for I cannot bear evidence to the distress of my people without bearing evidence to the oppression and high-handedness of the landlord and his factor ... The principal thing we complain of is our poverty. The smallness of our holdings and the poor quality of the land are what has caused our poverty, and the way in which the poor crofters are huddled together, and the best part of the land devoted to deer forests and big [sheep] farms... The remedy throughout the island of Skye is easy to supply – give us land out of the plenty that there is about for cultivation. Give us land at a suitable rent – at a rent within our power to pay.

▼ Source 3

Donald McLeod of Glenelg, Inverness told the Commission this:

Sixteen years ago I reclaimed two and a half acres of land; since then I have built a barn, byre and stable and built an addition to our dwelling house which our father built. I spent more money on the property than any other crofter in it. Five years ago the present factor Mr Mollisson in June 1878, took from me the largest half of my croft, and charged me £10, 10 shillings [£10.50p] for the remaining half. [The rent for the whole croft had been £14.]

▼ Source 4

John MacLeod, boatbuilder, Lionel, Ness, Isle of Lewis.

A larger harbour should be built here and they should get large boats. Now all these men have to go to the east coast, and be under masters who can do with them as they like, and they [the local men] have not even one net of their own.

▼ Source 5

"We had a great reason to complain. About forty years ago there were twenty-four crofts in this village, and now it is situated on forty-eight, with heavy families.'

This evidence is from the North Boisdale crofter representative. He drew attention to 'sub-dividing' crofts between family members.

The practice of sub-dividing meant the amount of crofting land decreased for each generation because no new land was made available. It was a problem common to all crofting townships.

▼ Source 6

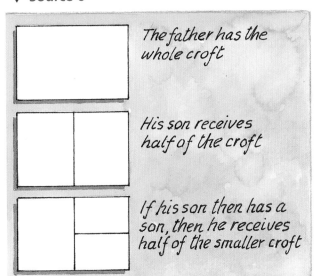

The father has the whole croft

His son receives half of the croft

If his son then has a son, then he receives half of the smaller croft

The Napier Commission recommendations did not please the crofting community. Unrest and rent strikes continued. In 1885, five crofter Members of Parliament were elected. In 1886 a Crofters Act was passed. It largely ignored the Napier Commission recommendations. It represented a great achievement, but was only intended as a short-term solution to the Highlands.

▼ Source 7

Recommendations and results.

The demands of the Highland Land League Reform Association	What the Napier Commission recommended	What the Crofters Act 1886 said
Fair rents. Security of tenure. Compensation for improvements.	Planned phasing out of all crofts under 6 acres. This would end the existence of the cottars.	Security of tenure as long as rent paid. This meant an end to to oldstyle mass clearances.
The land used for deer and sheep to be given back to the people.	The cottars and even some crofters would be encouraged to emigrate. The government should assist crofters to buy their own crofts rather than offer them security of tenure for evermore.	Fair rent to be ensured by a Crofters Commission (government body). A right to compensation for improvements in the event of the croft being given up.

1 Make a list of the problems faced by the crofting population from Sources 2, 3, 4, 5 and 6.

2 Look at Source 7:
   a What would the crofters have been delighted with?
   b What would they have been disappointed with?

3 The cottars were especially disappointed. A number of land raids followed. Can you suggest why from Source 7?

4 What do you think are the advantages and disadvantages of eye-witness accounts to the historian?

A C T I V I T I E S

Leaving for the Forces

At the Battle of Culloden (16 April 1746), the Highland clans who fought for Bonnie Prince Charlie were defeated. However, the Highland soldier had shown his fighting ability and bravery. A terrifying 'Highland Charge' was used against the enemy. At the battle of Prestonpans (21 September 1745), the government forces of Sir John Cope fled in terror, as the Highlanders charged downhill towards them. At Culloden, even after suffering heavy casualties from 45 minutes of artillery shelling, the Highland clans charged at a much larger army, into the face of sleet and a hail of 'grapeshot' and musket balls. Culloden was the end of Jacobite rebellions in the Highlands. The problem for chiefs and government was now what to do with such 'warlike' Highlanders.

▼ **Source 1**

I should imagine that two or three independent Highland companies might be of use; they are hardy, intrepid, accustomed to a rough country, and no great mischief if they fall.

General Wolfe fought against the Highlanders at Culloden. He and other officers convinced the government that the Highlander could be used to fight for the British army, in their wars abroad. He was a good soldier, but 'expendable'.

▼ **Source 2**

If I raise a regiment for the government this will prove my loyalty. I will also receive payment for each soldier who enlists. I have no need for warlike clansmen in my property to fight other clans, because the clan system is now dead. My own regiment will show my importance to other landowners.

This sums up the view of chiefs in the period after Culloden. They were starting to think increasingly as landowners.

▼ **Source 3**
Highland soldier of the Black Watch, 1744.

The Black Watch had been the first Highland Regiment to fight abroad for the British army. They were formed in 1725 from the clansmen of Highland chiefs opposed to the Jacobites. Their job was to police the Highlands and warn the government of any further unrest. A further 12 Highland regiments were raised between 1756 and 1763. They fought against the French in Canada, Europe and India. Many stories of bravery quickly gave Highland Regiments a world-wide reputation.

▲ Source 4
This painting shows a scene from the battle of Vimiera, 1808. It shows a piper of the 11th Highland Regiment.

After enlisting, an ordinary soldier had to face many dangers, apart from just the enemy. Being shipwrecked was a real possibility.

▼ Source 5
An eye-witness account from one of the eight surviving soldiers after the sinking of the Birkenhead, 26 February 1852.

Until the vessel disappeared there was not a cry or a murmur from the soldiers or sailors. Those who could swim struck out for the shore, but few ever reached it; most of them either sank from exhaustion, or were devoured by sharks, or were dashed to death on the rugged shore near Danger Point, or were entangled in the deathgrip of the long arms of seaweed.

Another danger was disease caused by the poor standard of hygiene, both on board ship during the voyage and during campaigns. Despite the hardships, Highland regiments were well thought of for their all-round good behaviour and had very few mutinies, or beatings. There is evidence that by the time of the Crimean War against Russia, Highlanders were less willing to volunteer for service. An old man expressed his opinion to the Duke of Sutherland during a recruitment drive.

▼ Source 6

We could not expect worse treatment than we have experienced at the hands of your family for the last fifty years. How could your Grace expect to find men where they are not, and the few of them which are to be found amongst the rubbish or ruins of the country, have more sense than to be decoyed [lured into a trap] by chaff [good-humoured teasing] to the field of slaughter.

This story was told to Donald MacLeod by someone else. MacLeod admits it may have been altered. Choose any word you think has been added to make it sound more dramatic.

1 Look at Source 4. What do you think has just happened to the piper in the painting? Give a reason for your answer. Remember, there is a battle going on!

2 Why do you think the piper is shown as wanting to continue playing?

3 Look at Sources 4 and 5. Do you think eye-witness accounts are more useful than a painting for finding out about Highland soldiers? Give reasons for your answer.

4 Look again at the painting of the piper. Let's suppose you want to check if what is shown actually happened or not. What sorts of evidence would you need to find? Give a reason for each of your choices.

5 How valuable is Source 6 for finding out about changing attitudes amongst Highlanders towards being a soldier in the British army? Explain your answer.

A C T I V I T I E S

Leaving for the City

By the close of the eighteenth century, it was possible to attend a Gaelic church service in Edinburgh, Glasgow, Dundee, Perth and Aberdeen. In 1790s Greenock, almost 3 in 10 of the entire population had been born in the Highlands. Highlanders appeared in such large numbers in towns and cities that Highland Societies quickly sprang up, including one in London from 1778.

This table shows the number of those born in the Highlands, living in some of the Lowland towns and cities in 1851.

▼ Source 1

Place and number of Highlanders in 1851.

Place	Number
Edinburgh	1,200
Glasgow	16,534
Greenock	4,200
Paisley	1,600

Many more Highlanders emigrated than ever moved to the growing urban centres of late eighteenth and nineteenth century Lowland Scotland. Working in a city or town was a poor second choice and was seen by many Highlanders as temporary. Living in a town or city was first and foremost, like seasonal migration, a means to pay for and keep their occupation of poor quality croft land, in the Highlands.

▼ Source 2

A very large number of the able-bodied men, especially in Ardnamurchan ... leave their wives and families for a great proportion of the year, go to Glasgow where they get employment in Dye Works and return to their possessions for only a few months in the summer. In most cases, these parties pay their rents well.

This is from a report in 1852. How does it help support the idea that Highlanders thought the croft land they occupied to be of great importance?

Permanent settlement in the towns and cities of Scotland became increasingly common after the 1850s, with growing job opportunities and further clearance and eviction after the 1846 potato famine.

This table shows the main jobs Highlanders worked at in Lowland towns and cities. The details are taken from nineteenth century census reports.

▼ Source 3

Occupations of Highlanders in Lowland Scotland.

Place	Male jobs	Female jobs
Glasgow	police; shipbuilding; construction; fishing; metalworking; machinery	domestic service
Edinburgh	police; porters; labourers (e.g. Edinburgh – Berwick railway); chairmen (sedan trade); shopmen	domestic service
Greenock	fishing; joinery; cooperage	domestic service
Dundee	general labouring	linen and jute mills

By the late eighteenth century, Edinburgh's sedan trade was dominated by Highlanders. This allowed the wealthy to be carried to their destination in the city.

▲ **Source 4**
Sedan chair.

Many migrant Highlanders were skilled or semi-skilled. This meant their standard of living was better than the unskilled Irish migrant. However, some of the poorest Highlanders did live in the worst slum areas of Glasgow.

This is from a medical officer's report in 1848.

▼ **Source 5**

Glasgow houses are so lofty the direct light of the sky never reaches a large part of the dwellings. There are large dunghills near the windows and doors, until farmers can be bargained with for their removal. The sewers, where they exist, are pools polluting the air. I saw a backyard covered with several inches of green putrid water ... There are no domestic conveniences [toilets] even in the tallest tenements except a kind of wooden sink outside some stair window and joined by a square wooden pipe with the surface of the court beneath. Down it is poured the entire filth of the households.

▲ **Source 6**
Close No. 80, High Street, Glasgow, 1868.

This is Close No. 80, High Street, Glasgow 1868. It was one of the city's worst slum areas. How can you tell this is an overcrowded area? Can you spot one improvement since the medical officer's report in 1848 (Source 5)?

Diseases continued to be a problem throughout the nineteenth century. Working conditions could be harsh too, with long hours and low pay. Only conditions in David Dale and Robert Owen's cotton mill at New Lanark were exceptions to this rule. This mill had workers from Caithness, Barra and Skye.

For the poorest Highlanders, in particular, faced with poor living and working conditions in the city, even this was better than complete poverty back in the Highlands.

1 Imagine you are a Highlander in the middle of the nineteenth century.

2 Draw up a list of 'pros and cons' about moving to the city. Use the text and sources on both these pages to help you.

A C T I V I T I E S

Emigrating

Historical Evidence

These two pages contain different sorts of ways of finding out about the past. Look at all the sources carefully.

1 Make a list of the different sorts of evidence you can see here. For example, one sort is an artist's sketch.

2 Can you suggest any other useful sources for finding out about emigrating?

3 Read Sources 2 and 3 carefully. How do these two sources differ when describing life on board an emigrant ship?

4 What evidence can you find in Source 4 to support the idea that this emigrant was not as wealthy as the person in Source 3?

5 Look at Source 6. Despite the possible hardships, what was the one overwhelming reason for choosing to emigrate?

6 Look at all the sources of evidence on these pages. Which one is the more valuable for someone wanting to find out about life on board an emigrant ship? Give reasons for your choice and explain why you rejected the others.

with our sails split, our rigging damaged and the ship quite disorganised ... a male child was born yesterday during the height of the storm ... we have fever, smallpox and measles on board ... The cries of the women last night were truly distressing.

▼ **Source 1**
Newspaper advertisement for emigration to Sydney.

EMIGRATION.

**FROM GREENOCK,
FOR SYDNEY, NEW SOUTH WALES.**

THE fine A 1 Poop Ship HERALD (a regular trader), 911 tons register, J. B. COUBRO, Commander, will be despatched 20th September, with Bounty Emigrants, under the regulations of Her Majesty's Emigration Commissioners. A Free Passage in the Steerage, with Provisions and Bedding, will be granted to a limited number of Married Agricultural Labourers, Shepherds, Carpenters, Smiths, Wheelwrights, Bricklayers, and Masons, (*for whom the most urgent demand exists in the Colony,*) provided they be of competent skill, good character, and accompanied by their wives ; also to Unmarried Female Domestic and Farm Servants, between the ages of 15 and 30, and a few Unmarried Young Men, of the classes above-named, between the ages of 18 and 30, *proceeding under the care of Married Persons.* A payment of Twenty Shillings will be required from each Statute Adult.

Persons desirous of obtaining the advantage of a free passage, must address a letter to the Agent, stating name, age, and calling, of each proposed Emigrant, (including children,) on receipt of which they will be informed whether the proposed Emigrants are probably eligible for a free passage, and be furnished with printed forms of application. As the HERALD will be the only Ship this season from the Clyde with Free Emigrants, early application is necessary.

Carries an Experienced Surgeon, appointed by Her Majesty's Commissioners.

For freight, and Cabin passage, having elegant Poop accommodation, apply to

J. D. SHEPPARD,
Emigration Office, 57, Buchanan Street.
Glasgow, 1st Aug., 1843.

People from the island of Tiree sailed on this ship in 1847. Which words in the description would make an emigrant less worried about the voyage?

◀ **Source 2**
A letter written from HMS Hercules at anchor off Rothesay, Isle of Bute, 30 Dec. 1852.

If you had been on board this ship and kept a diary, what sort of entry would you have made for this day?

Saturday 1st November 1863
I thought I would sit in my cabin for a while and write the particulars of the voyage . . . The hot bottle is very comfortable . . . we are fed very well, rather a sameness; roast pork, boiled shoulder and roast leg of mutton, curry and ham every day, plenty of pudding. The breakfasts are good.

Sunday 8th November
I make myself very comfortable with three flannel petticoats . . . Your underclothes don't get the least dirty but dresses do, there is so much wet about . . .

▲ Source 3

These are extracts from the diary of Mrs Murray Smith who returned to Britain for a holiday in 1864. Her parents had emigrated to Australia after 1800.

A London bookseller John Knox estimated, from his tour of the Highlands in the 1780s, that 20,000 people had emigrated between 1763 and 1775. Emigration continued throughout the next century, especially after the potato famine of the 1840s. Emigrating could be a very hard experience. Disease was a problem on a long sea voyage of many weeks, with no fresh food or water and poor hygiene.

The emigrant ship, *The Hector*, was bound for Pictou, Nova Scotia, Canada in 1773. Alexander MacKenzie gathered stories about the voyage from people in Nova Scotia. They were published in a book about the Clearances in 1883. (See Source 4.)

What can you see in the sketch below which suggests life on board an emigrant ship could be very unpleasant?

▼ Source 4

The ship was so rotten that the passengers could pick the wood out of her sides with their fingers. The accommodation was wretched, smallpox and dysentery broke out among the passengers. Eighteen of the children died, provisions became almost exhausted, the water became scarce and bad; the remnant of provisions left consisted mainly of salt meat, which, from the scarcity of water, added greatly to their sufferings. The oatcake carried by them became mouldy.

▼ Source 6

Here men fare well enough, with fine prosperous homes, something they would not see in their lifetime had they remained on the other side [Scotland] . . . The settlers have stone houses, brick houses, frame and log houses and most of those have an orchard, well branched, up to their eaves . . . This is a free land for people who suffered . . . in the country they left . . . They are free from . . . landlord . . . factor and baillie who used to harass them and bring the roof down over their heads.

This is from a song written by Hugh MacCorkindale and called 'Oran le seann lleach' (Song of an old Islayman in praise of Ontario).

▼ Source 5
This is an artist's view of life on board the emigrant ship HMS Hercules, 1852.

Highland emigrants in the eighteenth and nineteenth centuries were involved in the North American fur trade, the Canadian Pacific Railway, turning the American prairies into the world's most important food-producing area and probably inventing ice hockey, from their own game of shinty. Today, in Australia there are more than 70 Clan Societies. There were even two Creek Indian Chieftains, in North America, called MacIntosh and MacGillivray!

Large numbers of Scots, including Highlanders, also went to England. For those who emigrated, there could be a variety of experiences in their new life.

▼ Source 1
John MacLean left the island of Coll in 1819. He wrote 'Am Bard an Canada' (The Poet in Canada).

Before I fell all these lowering trees, and till the soil, and produce a crop, my arm's strength will have tired and failed before my children have come of age.

▼ Source 2

piles upon piles of unsightly coffins ... a melancholy mass of human suffering ... After passing through nearly two thousand adults ... you come to two or three hundred orphans, some only fifteen or twenty days old and many of them taken from the side, and some from the breast, of a dead mother.

Source 2 is from the observations of a Montreal man in 1847 who was on the island of Gross Ile, on the St Lawrence River, Canada. Gross Ile was used as a quarantine station for emigrants. It was reckoned there were 20,000 typhus victims present.

▼ Source 3
Extracts from emigrants' letters.

Alexander MacAllister, Cape Fear, America, 1760s:

You would do well to advise all poor people whom you wish well to take courage and come to this country.

W. P. MacKay, left Sutherland in 1847 for Adelaide, Australia:

Here is no starvation, no seizing of your goods for taxes, no begging for work, but plenty of good meat.

Angus MacDonald from Stornoway, Lewis, wrote from Australia in the 1880s:

There is not a better place in the whole world; there is not a better land under the sun than what it is here ... broke 14 acres of my land, and if I be spared I shall have 40 broke next year. I got a splendid ox and a good cow, and a heifer calf, plenty milk and butter, and plenty to eat of everything.

"RED" MACKENZIE AND NEW ZEALAND LAND REFORM

One of the Highlands' least known and yet most influential émigrés was John MacKenzie, who as Minister for Lands in New Zealand from 1891 – 1899 radically altered the future shape of that country by destroying the power of the land monopolists [landlords] and opening up the land to the people.

John MacKenzie was born into a Gaelic-speaking crofting family on the Ardross estate, a few miles from Alness, in 1838. Many of his relatives had already been cleared from the area and had settled in Canada and the USA. Such childhood experiences were to influence profoundly his political career, and one memory in particular was to remain vivid in his imagination until his death. He recalled as a child passing the local cemetery with his father on a wild wintry night and encountering a bedraggled group of dispossessed crofters huddling there for shelter with nowhere else to go.

With such a harsh upbringing, it is hardly surprising that he decided to emigrate and seek a better life in New Zealand. On May 23rd 1860, his wedding-day, he sailed from Glasgow for Otago on the 'Henrietta' with his bride, an Annie Munro from Glen Glass.

▲ **Source 4**
A recent article in the *West Highland Free Press* newspaper.

The Emigrants' Information Office in New Zealand reported on 1 October 1888:

The trade and labour [job] market of the Colony [New Zealand] are much depressed at the present time. There is practically no demand for artisans [handicraftsman] and mechanics, and only a moderate demand in certain districts for good agriculturalists.

Before the emigrants arrived in North America, Australia and New Zealand, the native peoples had occupied the land for centuries. Highland emigrants were amongst the Europeans who came to these countries and took the land for themselves.

▼ **Source 5**

Our natives have been much more quiet lately and I think every year they will become more accustomed to our ways if not civilised: they now begin to find out that powder is more deadly than their spears. It is common belief among them that all white people were at one time black, that they died and jumped up white people in England. I am claimed by two tribes as a brother.

D. S. Murray wrote this (Source 5) about the Aborigines of Australia in 1839. Other Highland emigrants described the Aborigines as savages. In New Zealand, the Maoris were also to lose their land to white emigrant settlers, including Highlanders. In Cape Breton, Canada, there are now two 'reservations' for the Micmac Indians. They inhabited the land before the arrival of Europeans.

1 Look at Sources 1 and 2. Make a list of the problems which an emigrant family could have faced after arrival in Canada.

2 Do you think anyone reading letters in newspapers, like those in Source 3, would have been encouraged to emigrate? Explain your answer.

3 Why could Source 4 lead to a 'biased' view when finding out about the lives of Highland emigrants in New Zealand?

4 In Source 5, what evidence is there to suggest that some Highland emigrants had little respect for the native peoples they met?

ACTIVITIES

The Struggle to Survive

Crofting after the 1880s

Study the information in this chapter and produce a report that answers the question: **Had crofting life improved by the early 1970s?**

Make a plan of what you hope to write. On the plan write down the main areas you want to cover in your report, together with any examples you want to use from any of the sources. Are there any other sources you can look at, either at home or at school? When you have prepared your report write it up neatly and illustrate it.

A C T I V I T I E S

Crofting was never intended to provide the people with a living from the land alone. At the time of the Clearances, crofts were deliberately kept too small to allow this to happen. The Crofters Act (1886) made no real attempt to transfer land from the deer and sheep farms of landowners to enlarge the size of crofts. Nor did the Act provide the Highlands with the means to create a greater number of jobs, which could to be combined with crofting. These two problems haunted the crofting community down to the twentieth century.

▼ **Source 1**
The Knoydart Land Raiders of 1948.

Source 1 shows the Knoydart Land Raiders of 1948. They are marking out new crofts.

Land raids continued in to the twentieth century and included the Uists, Tiree, Raasay and Skye. The Crofters Act (1886) had offered nothing to the poorest crofters, the cottars.

By the close of the 1920s, government bodies had brought overcrowding and landlessness, in the crofting communities, to an end. There were also improvements in living conditions.

▼ **Source 2**

We found that more attention is being paid to cultivation, to rotation of crops, to reclamation of outruns, to fencing and to the formation or repair of township roads; but most conspicuous of all the effects perceptible, is that upon buildings ... In a considerable number of localities we found new and improved houses and steadings erected by the crofters themselves since the passing of the Act.

This is from a government report in 1895. In what ways does it suggest that improvements had occurred by the close of the nineteenth century?

▼ **Source 3**
Houses below the official tolerable standard, 1972

Place	Percentage
North Uist	68
South Uist	58
Barra	74

Many of the houses inspected were thought to be totally unfit for living in. Why does this survey mean that the historian has to treat the findings of Source 2 with caution?

Between 1850 and 1950 the population of the Highlands fell by an estimated 100,000. Emigration and permanent migration to the towns and cities played key roles.

▲ **Source 5**
'A Highland Washing'.

▼ **Source 4**
From a government report of 1954.

The age distribution in many crofting townships has become unbalanced with the result that a very large proportion of the crofts are in the hands of old people. In such townships agricultural production suffers to a marked degree. It becomes difficult to secure the carrying out of the work of the township which must be done in common and a spirit of lethargy [unnatural sleepiness] tends to prevail ... Many holdings remain uncultivated.

Young people may also have been encouraged to leave the crofting communities because the way of life by the 1950s seemed old-fashioned and out of date, compared with the rest of the country. There was a distinct lack of leisure activities and places to go, even village halls.

Piped water was still unusual in crofting communities in the 1950s. The absence of things such as a kitchen sink, toilet and bathroom may explain why so few young girls decided to make a life in a crofting community in the early twentieth century.

▼ **Source 6**
Angus Og.

This is Angus Og, a cartoon character in a popular daily newspaper discovering a 'bothy' in Lewis. These were secret drinking dens where the men would go, because of the absence of pubs and clubs and the tendency of the church to take a dim view of drinking at all.

Only in the 1970s, did a real positive change in the fortunes of crofting start to occur.

Crofting Today

Crofting still has difficulties to face. Oil-related jobs, in the 1970s, provided opportunities for crofters in the Cromarty Firth, Kishorn (Wester Ross), Arnish (Lewis), Orkney and Shetland. Most of these have now disappeared. Government attempts to create major industry in the Highlands have now largely failed. None the less, the European Union, environmentalists and the UK government itself are now much more positive towards small farming combined with other jobs. There is some evidence to suggest that the range of 'other jobs' is now much wider than before.

Small mobile family businesses often provide a valuable service in the Highlands, because townships are so spread out and there are no big towns close by. You will find mobile banks, libraries, grocery and butcher vans.

▼ **Source 1**
An aerial view over the crofting township of Achiltibuie, Wester Ross. You can see the strips of cultivated land and hill pasture for animals.

These crofters are gathering hay. Crofting is mainly based on rearing livestock, with crops for winter feed and next season's seed. Recently, the number of sheep in crofting areas has increased as they require less management and subsidies are available.

▼ **Source 2**
Crofters near Leverburgh, Harris.

You are a historian preparing a report on the crofting community today.

Section 1 of your report should list the different types of evidence you intend to use. You should add other sources of evidence to those shown on these two pages. Explain the strengths and weaknesses of each source of evidence.

Section 2 of your report should list a number of questions you want to ask about changes that have happened and are continuing to happen now in crofting communities. For example, is there evidence to suggest more young people are choosing to remain in crofting communities? At the end of each question put the source of evidence you would use to get your answer, in brackets. (The following sources should help you with some questions, but you should also aim to add others from your own ideas).

Section 3 of your report should use the evidence on these two pages to make your first conclusions about crofting life today.

A C T I V I T I E S

▲ **Source 3**
Pig farming.

Some crofters are trying to find new ways of making crofting pay. This crofting family from Carinish, North Uist, have developed a very successful pig rearing business.

The 'buy out' of land by entire communities has happened in the 1990s. The community no longer has a landlord to worry about. The Island of Eigg is a recent example.

This is a modern croft house in Wester Ross. Its construction was helped with a crofters building grant of money. The owners offer Bed & Breakfast to tourists. Tourism has become a major industry in crofting areas. However, in the late 1980s the average crofter earning was only £8,000 per annum and in 1990 a government report found that the highest proportion of all housing with outside sanitation was in the Western Isles. This area also has an unemployment figure above the national average.

▼ **Source 4**
Modern crofter's house, Wester Ross.

SEAFOOD CRUISE

IMAGINE: Having the chance to eat the freshest, prized seafood, Langoustine, Queen scallops, Squat lobsters and Crab.
IMAGINE: A cruise around the waters of Lochalsh to Lochcarron enjoying the wildlife; seals, cormorants, porpoise and ducks.
We are offering a flexible service combing both. You will be picked up at a pier nearest to your accommodation and taken on a two hour cruise (approx.)

On the tour we will be picking up freshly caught shellfish from our fishing boat "The Green Isles" ("The Fat Chance" of Hamish Macbeth fame) which will be simply cooked and served with wine and salad.
This is a unique seafaring experience combining the natural scenic beauty of the area with the delicious produce of our unpolluted waters.

Our boat is a purpose built Starfish 8 with all life saving and safety equipment to M.S.A. standard and is equipped with a canopy for inclement weather should it arise.

▲ **Source 5**

West Coast fishing continues to face intense competition from much larger East Coast boats. Some prawn fishermen have recently given up and do tourist trips instead.

Fish farms are a new development to traditional industries such as tweed manufacture in the Outer Isles. However, some environmentalists are concerned about the impact of such 'farming' on the local habitat.

There is some evidence to suggest that the younger generation are remaining in greater numbers in crofting communities. This has led to an increased demand for crofts. However, in many crofting communities wealthy middle-class people from elsewhere have outbid local people for crofts.

A Heritage?

▲ **Source 1**
Mural from Pictou, Nova Scotia.

The story of the Highlands since 1746 is one which allows us to understand the forces which have changed people's lives. It also shows us how the Highland people themselves were able to contribute to the heritage of other areas, for example the Lowland towns and cities and countries abroad, such as Canada, America, Australia and New Zealand. If you visit the Highlands, you will find a large amount of evidence about the changes which have taken place. Some of that evidence is shown on these pages. How and why we remember the past is important. Someone once said, 'Those who forget history condemn the future'.

▼ **Source 2**

(CHORUS)

They did a Dance
Called America
They danced it round
And waited at the turns
For America
They danced their ladies round

Source 2 is from a song by a band called Runrig whose members all come from the Highlands. Their songs are in both Gaelic and English. The band has been very popular in the 1980s and 1990s. Some of their songs tell about events which have shaped the Highlands. The words are from one such song, 'Dance Called America'. The name was taken from two travellers to the Highlands (Dr Johnson and Mr Boswell) at the end of the eighteenth century, who saw this dance being performed by Highlanders waiting to emigrate.

▼ **Source 3**
Clearance site.

This clearance site is in Sutherland. If you walk around the site you will find plaques beside the ruins containing information.

▼ **Source 4**
Monument at Badbea.

This is a monument built at what was once a crofting site at Badbea. It is said on the information plaques that because the site was so high up on the clifftops, the people tied down their animals to prevent them from falling over the sheer drop, just yards away. It is also suggested that they did the same to their young children! The monument was erected by one of the emigrants' sons, with money earned from a new life in New Zealand.

▲ Source 6
Interior of a croft house museum, Isle of Lewis.

Museums like the one in Lochmaddy, North Uist, are also becoming more concerned with helping visitors, from places such as America, to trace where their ancestors came from.

▼ Source 5
Sign for the Gaelic College on the Isle of Skye.

The Gaelic College on the island of Skye recently gained permission for an expansion of its facilities. The growth in Gaelic television provision has been a major employer in recent years. Schools too have encouraged the teaching and learning through Gaelic. Road signs in some parts of the Highlands are provided in both Gaelic and English.

There are many museums in the Highlands. A visit to any one will tell you about the life and times of the area. Some museums now have information provided in more than one foreign language, such as French or German, to help visitors understand Highland history.

1 Why is it important to remember the experiences of the Highlands since the Battle of Culloden in 1746?

2 We call the reminders of the past, both physical and oral, our heritage. List all the ways in which we are reminded of the experiences of the Highland people from the sources above. Are there any other ways, not on these pages, which remind us also?

3 Is the preserving of the past important in your opinion? Which of the above examples of the past is the most important to preserve in your opinion? Why did you make that choice?

4 Look at Source 6. The kind of people who come to the Highlands might be interested in hill walking or rock climbing, but they also tend to be interested in Highland history. If you agree that preserving the past is important, can you suggest ways in which more people can become more aware of the events which have shaped Highland history since 1746? Explain your list of suggestions and discuss them with the rest of your class.

ACTIVITIES

Further Reading

R. Francis — *The Blood is Strong*. A novel of the Highland Clearances. House of Lochar 1997.

This novel transports a modern-day Canadian girl back in time to when there were evictions in the nineteenth century Uists.

R. Gibson — *Highland Clearances Trail: A Guide*. Highland Heritage Books, 1996.

This provides a basic guide to the location of clearance sites and monuments.

There are some very good non-fiction books about the clearances and crofting, but they all tend to have been written for adults.

Further Information

However, there are some excellent museums worth visiting to get an idea of Clearances and crofting life.

Ullapool Museum and Visitor Centre, 7 & 8 West Argyle Street, Ullapool IV26 2TY. This is my personal favourite. It has an audio-visual display, folders of photographs and documents, information on computer databases and is well laid out with interesting information boards.

Arnol Museum, Arnol, Lewis, is a reconstructed blackhouse with a peat fire burning in the centre and the sorts of goods to be found in such a croft house in the nineteenth century.